ARTHUR E. SUTHERLAND

THE CHURCH SHALL BE FREE

A GLANCE AT EIGHT CENTURIES OF CHURCH AND STATE

PUBLISHED FOR THE MAGNA CARTA COMMISSION
BY THE UNIVERSITY PRESS OF VIRGINIA, CHARLOTTESVILLE

The woodcut on the front cover of the murder of Thomas à Becket by knights of Henry II in 1170 first appeared in Caxton's English version (Westminster, c. 1484-85) of Jacobus de Voragine's *The Golden Legend*.

The Church Shall Be Free

A Glance at Eight Centuries

of Church and State

Magna Carta Essays
General Editor: A. E. Dick Howard

Published for
The Magna Carta
Commission
of Virginia

The Church Shall Be Free

A Glance at Eight Centuries of
Church and State

Arthur E. Sutherland

Bussey Professor of Law
Harvard University

The University Press of Virginia
Charlottesville

The Church Shall Be Free
A Glance at Eight Centuries
of Church and State

In the late twentieth century no intellectual feat is more difficult—or perhaps more clearly impossible—than transmuting today's concepts into those of a man living in 1215. One can only approximate what our predecessors thought seven and a half centuries ago. They spoke and wrote—the few who could write at all—in words now strange to most of us, and thinking depends largely on the meaning of words. What the "free English church" which John promised in the Great Charter[1]

[1]"[Q]uod Anglicana ecclesia libera sit, et habeat jura sua integra, et libertates suas illesas . . . ." Magna Carta, chap. 1 (W. S. McKechnie, *Magna Carta* [2d ed., reprint; New York, 1958], p. 190).

meant to the King and to those who received his promise, we can never exactly know. Perhaps those who wrote the words had no precise connotations in mind. Perhaps the great ecclesiastics at Runnymede tried only to express a vaguely conceived aspiration so to conduct the affairs of their ancient, widespread, intricate, religious polity in its complex coexistence with a society of feudal power that their Church might be free from interference outside their own hierarchy. At any rate a man of 1965 should certainly not confuse any idea inhering in John's words with the theory of the most conspicuous single statement of our day concerning the relation between government and religion in the United States:

Neither a state nor the Federal Government can set up a church. Neither can pass laws which aid one religion, aid all religions, or prefer one religion over another. Neither can force nor influence a person to go to or to remain away from church against his will or force him to profess a belief or disbelief in any religion. No person can be punished for entertaining or professing religious beliefs or disbeliefs, for church attendance or non-attendance. No tax in any amount, large or small, can be levied to support any religious activities or institutions, whatever they may be called, or whatever form they may adopt to teach or practice religion. Neither a state nor the Federal Government can, openly or secretly, participate in the affairs of any religious organizations or groups and *vice versa*. In the words of Jefferson, the clause against establishment of religion by law was intended to erect "a wall of separation between church and State."[2]

In the latter part of the past seven centuries we have

[2]A dictum of Mr. Justice Black in Everson v. Board of Education, 330 U.S. 1, 15-16 (1947).

drastically changed our attitude toward the relation of government to religion. To most of us today the thinking of Stephen Langton, John Wycliffe, Mary Tudor, Thomas Cranmer, Oliver Cromwell, or even John Wesley is in some ways beyond reach. To read in their minds much relevance to today's religious ideas would be like seeking the one-man-one-vote theory of the *1964 Reapportionment Cases*[3] in the mind of Simon de Montfort, of 1265; or expecting to find today's separation of powers in Montesquieu's *De l'Esprit des Loix* of 1748. In King John's day, and for centuries after him, the problem of relation between lay ruler and Church was how governing power should be shared between them. Somehow it has come about that in our time a problem of government is the means of excluding all religious influence whatever from the business of governing. We have come to find that *cuius regio eius religio* is a slogan inconsistent with the political equality of all men and inconsistent with the ideal of free inquiry wherever the mind may seek. This essay undertakes a brief speculation as to how, and possibly why, this remarkable metamorphosis has occurred.

The Middle Ages were ages of belief. Men feared God, as well as adored Him. He was forgiving to those who deserved to be forgiven and who made proper requests; He was stern toward and condemned to hell's torture those who deserved eternal punishment. In 1199, John, newly become King John when his brother Richard died, went to visit Richard's tomb in the Abbey Church

[3]Reynolds v. Sims, 377 U.S. 533 (1964); Lucas v. Fortyfourth General Assembly, 377 U.S. 713 (1964).

of Fontevrault. Hugh, Bishop of Lincoln, met King John there, pointed to the Last Judgment carved in the porch of the church, and showed John the kings among those condemned to perdition. John piously responded by pointing to more godly kings in the sculpture, whom heavenly angels were taking to eternal bliss. The new King told Bishop Hugh that he intended to emulate their worthy example.[4] Even if John was no edifying specimen of piety in his life, he must have feared God. At the end, in 1216, sick to death at Newark, his enemies increasing, his treasure lost when he had crossed the Welland quicksands, he gave ten pounds to a monastery for his soul's good and, one hopes, so died shriven.

God could prosper a king in battle, if the king knew how to gain His favor. In 1066, when William's host was waiting to embark for the conquest of England, the Duke prayed constantly in the St. Valery Church for a favoring wind; and on the morning of Hastings, William vowed to God that if the Almighty would grant him victory over Harold, the Conqueror would build a great church on the hill where Harold's standard then flew. And indeed, in due course, William the Conqueror there built the church he had promised.

God, that is to say, for men of the Middle Ages, was no Celestial Mechanic who had set the universe going on a predetermined plan and who had then stood aside to let it work according to His grand design. He was, on the contrary, a Person of emotions very like those of an earthly monarch, rewarding His friends and wrathfully punishing those who opposed His will. A king did

[4]Dean W. R. W. Stephens tells the story in his *The English Church* (London, 1916), II, 208-9.

well to cultivate God's favor, not only by making gifts to His Church and by favoring its consecrated servants, but also by insisting that the king's subjects give God proper honor. Church and monarch joined to govern rightly. And as Henry II found out in 1170 when some of his men killed Becket in Canterbury Cathedral, reasonable royal piety was essential to successful rule; flagrant offense to God could oblige a king to engage in conspicuous public penance. His shocked subjects could insist on it.

All this obviously required that a king be sure that he was well informed about orthodoxy, which was a comparatively simple matter most of the time in pre-Reformation Europe. But the Reformation introduced difficult questions as to what God wanted. Henry VIII split with Rome in 1534 (perhaps not wholly on grounds of abstract theological speculation); his children, Edward, Mary, and Elizabeth, succeeding him in turn, respectively agreed and disagreed and then again agreed with Henry's ideas, which produced Protestant martyrs under Mary and Catholic martyrs under Elizabeth. Logically enough on their own premises, no one of the Tudors advocated "freedom of religion" in our sense, in which men are let alone by government to go to heaven or go to hell in their own way. Men were martyred for their own good and "pour encourager les autres."

This process of persecution could, in case enough subjects disagreed with a king, produce a royal martyr instead of producing martyrs among the king's subjects. So English Puritan revolutionaries executed William Laud, Archbishop of Canterbury, in 1645, and decapitated King Charles himself in 1649. Meantime Puritans

had come across the Atlantic to found what is now
Massachusetts—not to allow freedom for other sectaries
but to have freedom to insist on their own orthodoxy.
In their Puritan theocracy they logically equated heresy
with sedition, and in their *Lawes and Libertyes,* published by the Massachusetts General Court in 1647, they
enacted the death penalty for any man who should "have
or worship any other God but the Lord God" or who
should "be a witch, that is . . . consult with a familiar
spirit." They added:

> If any person within this Jurisdiction whether Chris-
> tian or Pagan shall wittingly and willingly presume to
> BLASPHEME the holy Name of God, Father, Son or
> Holy-Ghost, with direct, express, presumptuous, or high-
> handed blasphemy, either by wilfull or obstinate denying
> the true God, or his Creation, or Government of the
> world: or shall curse God in like manner, or reproach
> the holy Religion of God as if it were but a politick
> device to keep ignorant men in awe; or shal utter any
> other kinde of Blasphemy of the like nature & degree
> they shall be put to death.[5]

Consistently with this faith, the stern Puritan fathers
hanged Mary Dyer on Boston Common in 1660 for her
persistence in proclaiming Quaker doctrine. If the civil
authority is the same as the ecclesiastical, one logically
concludes, there is risk in tolerating heretics. The second
Charles was too worldly, too sophisticated, to see this
risk so simply. "Lo, these are my good subjects of New
England," he said when he heard of the hangings; he

---

[5] *The Laws and Liberties of Massachusetts* (Cambridge, Mass.,
1929), p. 5. See generally Thomas Hutchinson, *The History of
the Colony and Province of Massachusetts-Bay,* ed. L. S. Mayo
(Cambridge, Mass., 1936), pp. 371-72.

sent peremptory word to his stiff-necked royal Governor Endicott to stop punishing Quakers.[6]

There were other ideas stirring which were to help end theocracy. During the Renaissance in Europe a revival of scientific studies had accompanied the revival in other branches of learning. The concept grew and spread that the universe was governed by an undeviating system of natural forces, which could be studied and understood. This vision of the cosmos, accepted slowly and doubtfully at first, sometimes seemed to conflict with established ideas of religion. In 1633 Galileo was for a time imprisoned by the Inquisition in Rome. But by the end of the seventeenth century Newton was enjoying high honor in England as Lucasian Professor at Cambridge; in 1703 he became president of the Royal Society; and his ripe years were supported by royal patronage which, somewhat surprising to our twentieth-century ideas of civil service, made him Master of the Mint!

Poets took up the theme of universal order and law, in place of divine esteem and pique, as ruling influences in the universe. Pope wrote of

> one stupendous whole,
> Whose body Nature is, and God the soul . . . .

He explained away unpleasant aspects of life:

> harmony not understood;
> All partial evil, universal good;
> And, spite of Pride, in erring Reason's spite,
> One truth is clear, *Whatever Is, Is Right.*[7]

[6]See Thomas J. Wertenbaker, *The Puritan Oligarchy* (New York, 1947), pp. 229-41.

[7]Alexander Pope, *An Essay on Man* (London, 1802), pp. 56, 57 (Epis. 1, ll. 267-68, 289-94).

Even lawyers took up this theme of God's will working like a great machine. Blackstone wrote in the introduction to his *Commentaries* in 1765:

> Thus when the supreme being formed the universe, and created matter out of nothing, he impressed certain principles upon that matter, from which it can never depart, and without which it would cease to be. When he put that matter into motion, he established certain laws of motion, to which all moveable bodies must conform. And, to descend from the greatest operations to the smallest, when a workman forms a clock, or other piece of mechanism, he establishes at his own pleasure certain arbitrary laws for it's direction; as that the hand shall describe a given space in a given time; to which law as long as the work conforms, so long it continues in perfection, and answers the end of it's formation.[8]

There were philosophical difficulties in this Cosmic Clock which had consequences for a Church-and-State combination. The Undeviating Mechanism made God responsible for evil as well as good in man, and this has always been difficult to understand. If there is evil in the world, but still whatever is, is right, then how can we condemn evil? If God, for His inscrutable reasons, has left men a free will to choose a good course or a bad course, and if God punishes man when he follows the latter and rewards him when he chooses the former, then government logically allies itself with Church; and for man's own happiness as well as the ruler's convenience, both seek to persuade and even compel man to righteousness. However, the business of divinely permissive misconduct takes some explaining. Blackstone was a great teacher

[8]William Blackstone, *Commentaries* (2d ed.; Oxford, 1766), I, *38.

but not quite able to explain the theory of man's tendency to evil. He stated the fact of man's choice and appeared to be satisfied to stop there:

[A]s man depends absolutely upon his maker for everything, it is necessary that he should in all points conform to his maker's will.

This will of his maker is called the law of nature. For as God, when he created matter, and endued it with a principle of mobility, established certain rules for the perpetual direction of that motion; so, when he created man, and endued him with free will to conduct himself in all parts of life, he laid down certain immutable laws of human nature, whereby that freewill is in some degree regulated and restrained, and gave him also the faculty of reason to discover the purport of those laws.[9]

As long as most of a king's subjects were unlettered peasants, who took the parson's word for religious matters, Church could ally itself with State, in theory if not as completely in practice, as it had in King John's day. Widespread literacy, however, was certain to set ordinary men to reading religious books and then to speculating about the underlying reasons of both institutions, State and Church. Governor William Berkeley of Virginia was gifted with foresight in 1671 when he wrote to the Lords Commissioners of Foreign Plantations: "I thank God, *there are no free schools* nor *printing,* and I hope we shall not have these hundred years; for *learning* has brought disobedience, and heresy, and sects into the world, and *printing* has divulged them, and libels against the best government. God keep us from both!"[10]

[9] *Ibid.,* pp. *39-40.
[10] 2 *Laws of Virginia* 517 (Hening 1823). The Governor was answering a series of "Enquiries" about affairs in Virginia.

No development in human institutions seems to proceed from a single impulse. The laicizing of eighteenth-century society cannot, in major part, be ascribed to diffusion of abstract philosophical books among woodsmen, sailors, or simple cobblers. Among all the four million inhabitants of the United States in the last quarter of that enlightening century, only a small proportion can have read Blackstone's *Commentaries* or Pope's *An Essay on Man;* and though Newton's *Optics* was in the Harvard library in 1723, and a complete set of his works, Latin and English, is listed in the 1773 catalogue, it is a fair estimate that only a few Americans can have been stimulated directly by his ideas. But common schooling had induced a considerable spread of literacy, and the prevailing Protestantism with its emphasis on individual thought, with its labored doctrinal preaching Sunday after Sunday in thousands of village churches, tended to the fragmentation of old sects and in time to the creation of scores of new ones.[11] Although voting in elections was widely limited to freeholders, land was easy to own in a pioneer country, and if a man wanted to express himself in politics he could do so. There was no equal protection clause in the Constitution of 1789, but in a new land largely peopled by refugees from unpleasant conditions in Europe, conditions many of which were religio-political in their nature, no hardy settler was likely to tolerate unequal treatment of himself predicated on some other man's religious ideas. Literacy, skepticism, religious individualism, and a widespread

[11]Governor Berkeley, in the same answer to the Lords Commissioners in 1671, wrote: "We have fforty eight parishes, and our ministers are well paid, and by my consent should be better *if they would pray oftener and preach less." Ibid.*

confidence in political self-direction, all were inconsistent with "establishment" of churches in the newly independent States.

During the colonial period all the States, except possibly Rhode Island,[12] had some measure of establishment, and all, by the outbreak of the Revolution, had granted some freedom of worship to a number of sects other than those established. The two—establishment and intolerance of dissent—are not necessarily coterminous, as the First Amendment was to suggest. A government can support a favored religion financially without penalizing dissenters. Massachusetts did both when she began as a Puritan theocracy; Connecticut went nearly as far; New Hampshire had somewhat less establishment and more freedom. New York supported the Anglican and Dutch Reformed churches by rates but proscribed Roman Catholic services between 1700 and 1775. New Jersey, Pennsylvania, and Delaware had mild Christian establishments. Maryland under the first Calverts attempted to tolerate Roman Catholics and Protestants alike, but Protestant King William revoked the Calvert charter in 1690 and the Maryland Assembly then established the Church of England with a levy of forty pounds of tobacco per taxpayer.

Virginia from its beginning had a Church of England establishment; other Protestants were generally though not always tolerated; Roman Catholics suffered some

[12]The colonial charters are all collected in F. N. Thorpe's *Federal and State Constitutions, Colonial Charters and Other Organic Laws* (Washington, D. C., 1909). A standard text is Sanford H. Cobb, *The Rise of Religious Liberty in America* (New York, 1902). See also Anson Phelps Stokes, *Church and State in the United States* (New York, 1950).

disabilities. The Carolinas and Georgia attempted Church of England establishments but granted a limited freedom of religion to others.

One who reads the new constitutions of the revolutionary States adopted in the first decade of national independence[13] must be struck by the drastically new tone of the provisions concerning religion. Few relics of the colonial establishments carried over into the new state constitutions; still fewer remnants remained of old restrictions on religious exercise or of disqualification for public functions because of religious affiliation. This sudden change in documents must have registered a change in men's ideas which had been developing for a long time. The change is all the more striking when one remembers that until 1868 there was no federal constitutional limitation on state religious involvement; States could do as they pleased about establishing religions.[14] They disestablished their churches because their people wanted it so. Virginia was a leader in this movement for religious freedom; Jefferson and Madison were conspicuous in its development. Their work is such a notable part of disestablishment and free religion in America that it deserves telling at a little length.

The Virginia story can begin with an Act of 1748 which fixed the annual salary of a parish minister of the established Anglican Church at sixteen thousand pounds of tobacco. As tobacco then had a current price of

[13]Connecticut made do with its 1662 charter until 1818; Rhode Island governed itself under its 1663 charter until 1842!

[14]Unless the guaranty of a republican form of government in Article IV, Section 4, would limit a radically theocratic establishment.

sixpence a pound, a parson was reasonably well off with four hundred pounds sterling a year. But in 1758 times were hard, and the colonial legislature passed the Two-Penny Act, permitting payment of tobacco taxes during a ten-month period at twopence per pound. The tobacco market rose; clergymen felt hurt at being tendered pay at the twopence rate! The Reverend James Maury sued for his pay at the old rate, and the Virginia court in 1763 held the Two-Penny Act invalid because it lacked royal approval. But when a jury was empaneled to assess the damages, a young country lawyer named Patrick Henry spoke so eloquently in favor of the resisting ratepayers that the jury brought in a verdict for a single penny! The *Parsons' Cause* was a *cause célèbre* of its day. The jury's nominal verdict was an indication of popular dislike of a clergy beneficed by taxation; it foretold disestablishment to come.

As every schoolboy knows, war with England began in 1775. On June 12, 1776, a "General Convention of Delegates and Representatives from the several counties and corporations of Virginia, held at the Capitol in the City of Williamsburg," enacted a Declaration of Rights,[15] which suggests by much of its language the Bill of Rights proposed in 1789 by the first Congress under the Constitution of the United States and approved by the necessary States in 1791. The sixteenth section of the 1776 Virginia Declaration is said to owe its final form to James Madison. It declares

That religion, or the duty which we owe to our CREATOR, and the manner of discharging it, can be directed only by reason and conviction, not by force or violence, and

[15] 9 *Laws of Virginia* 109 (Hening 1821).

therefore all men are equally entitled to the free exercise of religion, according to the dictates of conscience; and that it is the mutual duty of all to practise Christian forbearance, love, and charity, towards each other.[16]

In 1784 the General Assembly of Virginia repealed all laws which under the Crown had specially favored the Church of England.[17] Since that time Virginia has never had an established church. Still the idea persisted that the State should support Christianity generally, though without preference among its various organized churches. At the same session in 1784 a committee of the Virginia legislature reported favorably "A Bill establishing a provision for Teachers of the Christian Religion." Everyone was to be taxed for that purpose, but the taxpayer was to be empowered to designate the "society of Christians" which his money would benefit. If any taxpayers selected no such society, their money would be used "for the encouragement of seminaries of learning within the Counties" whence such sums arose. Madison and Jefferson eloquently opposed the measure. At George Mason's suggestion Madison drew a "Memorial and Remonstrance against Religious Assessments," which gained such abundant support that the legislators abandoned the effort to pass a bill imposing religious taxes.[18]

In 1777 Jefferson had drafted "A Bill for Establishing Religious Freedom," and in 1779 the bill was introduced in the Assembly. Madison now pressed for its passage,

[16]*Ibid.,* pp. 111-12.

[17]*Ibid.,* pp. 532, 536-37.

[18]The texts of the bill and of Madison's "Remonstrance" can conveniently be found in the Supplemental Appendix and the Appendix to Mr. Justice Rutledge's dissenting opinion in Everson v. Board of Education, 330 U.S. 1, 63-74 (1947).

and it became a law in October 1785. It deserves at least partial quotation:

I. WHEREAS Almighty God hath created the mind free; that all attempts to influence it by temporal punishments or burthens, or by civil incapacitations, tend only to beget habits of hypocrisy and meanness, and are a departure from the plan of the Holy author of our religion, who being Lord both of body and mind, yet chose not to . . . propagate it by coercions on either, as was in his Almighty power to do; that the impious presumption of legislators and rulers, civil as well as ecclesiastical, who being themselves but fallible and uninspired men, have assumed dominion over the faith of others, setting up their own opinions and modes of thinking as the only true and infallible, and as such endeavouring to impose them on others, hath established and maintained false religions over the greatest part of the world, and through all time; that to compel a man to furnish contributions of money for the propagation of opinions which he disbelieves, is sinful and tyrannical; that even the forcing him to support this or that teacher of his own religious persuasion, is depriving him of the comfortable liberty of giving his contributions to the particular pastor, whose morals he would make his pattern, and whose powers he feels most persuasive to righteousness, and is withdrawing from the ministry those temporary rewards, which proceeding from an approbation of their personal conduct, are an additional incitement to earnest and unremitting labours for the instruction of mankind; that our civil rights have no dependence on our religious opinions, any more than our opinions in physics or geometry; that therefore the proscribing any citizen as unworthy the public confidence by laying upon him an incapacity of being called to offices of trust and emolument, unless he profess or renounce this or that religious opinion, is depriving him injuriously of those privileges and advantages to which in common with his fellow-citizens he has a natural right . . . .

II. *Be it enacted by the General Assembly, That no* man shall be compelled to frequent or support any religious worship, place, or ministry whatsoever, nor shall be enforced, restrained, molested, or burthened in his body or goods, nor shall otherwise suffer on account of his religious opinions or belief; but that all men shall be free to profess, and by argument to maintain, their opinion in matters of religion, and that the same shall in no wise diminish, enlarge, or affect their civil capacities.

III. And though we well know that this assembly elected by the people for the ordinary purposes of legislation only, have no power to restrain the acts of succeeding assemblies, constituted with powers equal to our own, and that therefore to declare this act to be irrevocable would be of no effect in law; yet we are free to declare, and do declare, that the rights hereby asserted are of the natural rights of mankind, and that if any act shall be hereafter passed to repeal the present, or to narrow its operation, such act will be an infringement of natural right.[19]

As the 1780's passed, the intolerable weaknesses of the Articles of Confederation became obvious, and the Convention of 1787 drafted a new Constitution for the United States. When eleven of the thirteen States ratified the Constitution in late 1787 and in 1788, five of them indicated that they accepted the Constitution on the understanding that it would be amended by the addition of a Bill of Rights. The States were nervous about entrusting too much power to a central government; its possible power over religion was one of the causes of concern. Virginia's recitals included a statement that "among

[19] 12 *Laws of Virginia* 84-86 (Hening 1823).

other essential rights, the liberty of conscience and of the press cannot be cancelled, abridged, restrained or modified by any authority of the United States."[20]

Madison was elected to the first House of Representatives, and on June 8, 1789, he proposed to the House a series of constitutional amendments, most of which, somewhat modified in form, were approved by Congress and became the present Bill of Rights. Two of Madison's proposals particularly concern the relation of Church and State: "The civil right of none shall be abridged on account of religious belief or worship, nor shall any national religion be established, nor shall the full and equal rights of conscience be in any manner, or on any pretext, infringed."[21] This clause was intended, one gathers, as a restraint only on the national government, for Madison proposed a correlative restraint on the States, telling the House, "I think there is more danger of those powers being abused by the State Governments than by the Government of the United States."[22] History proved Madison right. Whatever be the reasons, the principal controversies over religion in government which arose during the following century and three-quarters have concerned state measures. Madison's state proposal read, "No State shall violate the equal rights of conscience, or the freedom of the press, or the trial by jury in criminal cases."[23]

---

[20]*Debates and Proceedings of the Convention of Virginia,* ed. David Robertson (2d ed.; Richmond, 1805), p. 469. See also Irving Brant, *James Madison* (Indianapolis, 1941-61), I, 250.

[21]1 *Annals of Congress* 434 (1789).

[22]*Ibid.,* p. 440.

[23]*Ibid.,* p. 435.

But the Congress of 1789 was not greatly concerned with putting limits on the States. In that year, when the central government was still new and strange, men were worried lest their local autonomy be overridden by a distant, powerful, unfamiliar polity, perhaps dominated by the large States, of which Virginia was much the largest and most influential. No accident brought it about that in the forty years from Washington's inauguration in 1789 to the end of John Quincy Adams' term in 1829, four of the six Presidents, who held office for thirty-two of those forty years, came from the Virginia gentry. State representation in the Electoral College is largely proportionate to the popular vote,[24] and Virginia was far and away the most populous State in the Union. Some of the same concern shown by the smaller States during the Constitutional Convention of 1787 lest they be overborne by the new national government is reflected in the Bill of Rights. At any rate, Madison's proposal that the new national government protect men against deprivation by their own States of freedom of religion, of free expression, and of trial by jury never got through the Senate. But his proposed amendment concerning limits on national religious activity now appears as the first clause of the First Amendment: "Congress shall make no law respecting an establishment of religion, or prohibiting the free exercise thereof . . . ."

So well have men remembered Madison's part in shaping this guaranty and his preceding pronouncements on

[24]"Each State shall appoint, in such manner as the Legislature thereof may direct, a Number of Electors, equal to the whole Number of Senators and Representatives to which the State may be entitled in the Congress . . . ." U. S. Constitution, Art. II, Sec. 1, Cl. 2.

Canterbury Cathedral, where Thomas à Becket was martyred in 1170.
(Courtesy of the British Information Services)

Thomas Jefferson, author of the Bill for Establishing Religious Freedom.
(Courtesy of the Library of Congress)

A BILL *for eftablifhing* RELIGIOUS FREEDOM, *printed for the confideration of the* PEOPLE.

WELL aware that the opinions and belief of men depend not on their own will, but follow involunta-
rily the evidence propofed to their minds, that Almighty God hath created the mind free, and
manifefted his Supreme will that free it fhall remain, by making it altogether infufceptible of
reftraint: That all attempts to influence it by temporal punifhments or burthens, or by civil incapacitations, tend only to beget habits of hypocrify and meannefs, and are a departure from the plan of the holy
author of our religion, who being Lord both of body and mind, yet chofe not to propagate it by coercions on
either, as was in his Almighty power to do, but to extend it by its influence on reafon alone: That the impious
prefumption of legiflators and rulers, civil as well as ecclefiaftical, who, being themfelves but fallible and unin-
fpired men, have affumed dominion over the faith of others, fetting up their own opinions and modes of thinking, as the only true and infallible, and as fuch, endeavouring to impofe them on others, hath eftablifhed and
maintained falfe religions over the greateft part of the world, and through all time: That to compel a man
to furnifh contributions of money for the propagation of opinions which he difbelieves and abhors, is finful and
tyrannical: That even the forcing him to fupport this or that teacher of his own religious perfuafion, is
depriving him of the comfortable liberty of giving his contributions to the particular paftor whofe morals he
would make his pattern, and whofe powers he feels moft perfuafive to righteoufnefs, and is withdrawing from
the miniftry thofe temporal rewards which, proceeding from an approbation of their perfonal conduct, are
an additional incitement to earneft and unremitting labour for the inftruction of mankind: That our civil
rights have no dependance on our religious opinions, any more than our opinions in phyficks or geometry:
That therefore the profcribing any citizen as unworthy the publick confidence, by laying upon him an
incapacity of being called to offices of truft and emolument, unlefs he profefs or renounce this or that religious
opinion, is depriving him injurioufly of thofe privileges and advantages to which, in common with his fellow
citizens he has a natural right: That it tends alfo to corrupt the principles of that very religion it is meant
to encourage, by bribing with a monopoly of wordly honours and emoluments, thofe who will externally
profefs and conform to it: That though indeed thefe are criminal who do not withftand fuch temptation,
yet neither are thofe innocent who lay the bait in their way: That the opinions of men are not the object of
civil government, nor under its jurifdiction: That to fuffer the civil Magiftrate to intrude his powers into the
field of opinion, and to reftrain the profeffion or propagation of principles on fuppofition of their ill tendency,
is a dangerous fallacy, which at once deftroys all religious liberty; becaufe he being of courfe judge of that
tendency will make his own opinions the rule of judgment, and approve or condemn the fentiments of others
only as they fhall fquare with, or differ from his own: That it is time enough for the rightful purpofes of
civil government for its officers to interfere when principles break out into overt acts againft peace and good
order: And finally, That truth is great and will prevail if left to herfelf; that fhe is the proper and fufficient
antagonift to error, and has nothing to fear from the conflict, unlefs by human interpofition, difarmed of her
natural weapons, free argument and debate; errours ceafing to be dangerous when it is permitted freely to
contradict them

WE the General Affembly of *Virginia* do enact, that no man fhall be compelled to frequent or fupport
any religious Worfhip place or Miniftry whatfoever, nor fhall be enforced, reftrained, molefted, or burthened
in his body or goods, nor fhall otherwife fuffer on account of his religious opinions or belief, but that all men
fhall be free to profefs, and by argument to maintain their opinions in matters of religion, and that the fame
fhall in no wife diminifh, enlarge, or affect their civil capacities.

AND though we well know that this Affembly, elected by the people for the ordinary purpofes of legiflation
only, have no power to reftrain the acts of fucceeding Affemblies, conftituted with powers equal to our own,
and that therefore to declare this act irrevocable would be of no effect in law; yet we are free to declare, and
do declare, that the rights hereby afferted are of the natural rights of mankind, and that if any act fhall be
hereafter paffed to repeal the prefent, or to narrow its operation, fuch act will be an infringement of natural
right.

*The earlieft printed text of the Bill for Eftablifhing Religious
Freedom, 1785. (Courtefy of the Bofton Public Library)*

*Original draft of James Madison's "Memorial and Remonstrance,"
1784. (Courtesy of the Library of Congress)*

separation of State and religion that a century and a half later the Justices of the Supreme Court have seemed almost to be treating Madison's political writings as governing canons, fixing the meaning of the First Amendment, and derivatively the Fourteenth (whose Due Process and Equal Protection Clauses now "incorporate" the provisions of the First), and in effect writing in the Constitution the guaranty "that no State shall violate the equal rights of conscience" which Madison proposed to the House on the eighth of June, 1789.[25]

But this development of national protection from state control of religion was a long time coming. The words of the First Amendment are prohibitions explicitly against congressional action. Indeed, commentators have pointed out that those New England States which continued their Congregational establishments after the Revolution may have favored the form in which the First Amendment was finally adopted precisely because it categorically forbade Congress to legislate against the surviving Puritan formulas in their state governments,[26] and these States wished to protect what they had. The first ten amendments had a strong States' rights flavor. This was forcibly demonstrated in 1833 when the Supreme Court held that a State which confiscated private property for public use was not obliged by the Fifth

---

[25]See, e.g., Justices Black and Rutledge in Everson v. Board of Education, 330 U.S. 1, 11-13, 31, 33-34, 51-57 (1947); Justice Reed in Illinois ex rel. McCollum v. Board of Education, 333 U.S. 203, 244, 247-48 (1948); and Justice Douglas in Engel v. Vitale, 370 U.S. 421, 444 (1962).

[26]See Joseph M. Snee, S. J., "Religious Disestablishment and the Fourteenth Amendment," 1954 *Washington University Law Quarterly* 371, 388.

Amendment's Eminent Domain Clause or by anything else in the Federal Constitution to pay for what it had taken.[27] And a regrettable church quarrel in New Orleans showed in 1845 that the First Amendment put no limit on state interference in religious affairs. A municipal ordinance in that city penalized by fine any priest who should celebrate a funeral in certain Roman Catholic churches—a sort of limited interdict—and confined such services to an obituary chapel on Rampart Street. Father Permoli, fined for conducting funeral services in a proscribed church, went all the way to the Supreme Court of the United States in an effort to demonstrate that this interference exceeded the powers of a Louisiana city. Justice Catron disillusioned him. The Justice wrote in the Court's opinion: "The Constitution makes no provision for protecting the citizens of the respective states in their religious liberties; this is left to the state constitutions and laws: nor is there any inhibition imposed by the Constitution of the United States in this respect on the states."[28]

The Civil War of 1861-65 made much more profound changes in the relations between nation and States than was realized at the time. Mr. Justice Miller in the opinion of the Supreme Court in the *Slaughter-House Cases* of 1873 predicted that the Equal Protection Clause of the Fourteenth Amendment, then only five years old, would be applied only in racial matters:

We doubt very much whether any action of a State not directed by way of discrimination against the negroes as

[27]Barron v. Baltimore, 32 U.S. (7 Pet.) 243 (1833).

[28]Permoli v. Municipality No. 1, 44 U.S. (3 How.) 589, 609 (1845).

a class, or on account of their race, will ever be held to come within the purview of this provision. It is so clearly a provision for that race and that emergency, that a strong case would be necessary for its application to any other.[29]

But the Justice reckoned without some of the considerations which James Madison had so eloquently asserted in his unforgotten "Memorial and Remonstrance" of 1784. He and those many other objectors who subscribed to his protest against religious assessments had remonstrated against them

Because, the bill violates that equality which ought to be the basis of every law, and which is more indispensable, in proportion as the validity or expediency of any law is more liable to be impeached. If "all men are by nature equally free and independent," all men are to be considered as entering into Society on equal conditions; as relinquishing no more, and therefore retaining no less, one than another, of their natural rights. Above all are they to be considered as retaining an "equal title to the free exercise of Religion according to the dictates of conscience." Whilst we assert for ourselves a freedom to embrace, to profess and to observe the Religion which we believe to be of divine origin, we cannot deny an equal freedom to those whose minds have not yet yielded to the evidence which has convinced us . . . . [30]

Madison had gone on to protest that

the proposed establishment is a departure from that generous policy, which, offering an asylum to the persecuted and oppressed of every Nation and Religion,

[29]83 U.S. (16 Wall.) 36, 81 (1873).

[30]James Madison, *Letters and Other Writings* (Philadelphia, 1865), I, 164.

promised a lustre to our country, and an accession to the number of its citizens.[31]

As the last quarter of the nineteenth century arrived, larger and faster steamships were bringing more and more millions of new residents from foreign shores to the United States. Between 1860 and 1900 our population grew from thirty-one to seventy-five millions, and almost a third of these were immigrants. Great numbers were Roman Catholics, but substantial groups of north-western European Protestants and eastern European Jews added to the total. All these, like their millions of predecessor immigrants, were energetic people, self-selected for the qualities of initiative and courage necessary to come to a new country, and by the same tokens unwilling to submit to religious or political inequality. When Catholics found other population groups suspicious and "difficult," they built their own systems of parochial schools. They felt some injustice at paying taxes to support public schools, in many of which occurred Protestant Bible reading and prayers, while the Catholic parent had to bear the added expense of the parochial-school instruction of his children. Catholics exerted political pressure for public contributions to parochial-school costs, arousing fear of religio-political forces and evoking in 1875 the proposed Blaine Amendment to the Federal Constitution, which would have prohibited the use of state funds for any religious sect. It passed the House by 180 to 7; though it failed to get the required majority in the Senate,[32] the House vote demonstrated a strong current of political emotion.

[31]*Ibid.*, p. 166.

[32]See F. W. O'Brien, "The Blaine Amendment, 1875-1876," 41 *University of Detroit Law Journal* 137 (1963).

In 1878 the Supreme Court, considering the difficult question of religious observances which are violations of social inhibitions generally supported and which are therefore penalized by the criminal law, held that Mormons were not excused by their faith from legal penalties attaching to plural marriage.[33] Clearly the issue of Church and State in a constitutional democracy can arise in many different ways. But most of the twentieth-century Church-State constitutional controversies in the United States have concerned some aspect of religion in relation to common schools. In *Pierce v. Society of Sisters,* decided in 1925,[34] the Supreme Court held unconstitutional under the Due Process Clause of the Fourteenth Amendment an Oregon statute which required all young children to attend the public schools and which would thus have made impossible the conduct of private grade schools, religious or other. What of the converse case; some sort of public subvention for the education of all children which incidentally aids parochial schools to maintain themselves? In 1930 the Supreme Court, in *Cochran v. Louisiana State Board of Education,*[35] passed on the constitutionality of a Louisiana statute which provided, at public expense, free textbooks on lay subjects for all school children whether they used the books at public or parochial schools. The plaintiff, a taxpayer, claimed to be aggrieved by expenditure of tax proceeds for nonpublic purposes; he argued that this deprived him of his property without due process of law in violation of the Fourteenth Amendment. He set up no claim of un-

[33]Reynolds v. United States, 98 U.S. 145 (1878).

[34]268 U.S. 510 (1925).

[35]281 U.S. 370 (1930).

constitutional intermingling of Church and State. The Court, in an opinion by Chief Justice Hughes, found no violation of constitutional right. Education, the Chief Justice wrote, was a public purpose, and the taxpayer was not wronged when his money was so used.

Thus *Cochran* did not squarely meet the issue of constitutionality, *vel non,* of spending public funds, admittedly for purposes which the States are accustomed to aid but which may in some instances give incidental help to religious institutions. In a society with so many hundreds of years of religious history there are inevitably hosts of religious organizations—churches, hospitals, schools, colleges, universities, orphanages—institutions of the sort supported a few centuries ago by the established church of whatever country but now privately sponsored. Inevitably the social services of any State which is rapidly extending its activities for the general welfare will aid such religious institutions along with other private charities having no ecclesiastical link. The town fire department serves alike to put out a fire at St. Swithin's School for Boys or at the Grangedale Country Day School; the firemen do not stop to ask whether St. Swithin's is supported by a church. The police protect both; the municipal waterworks serve both. If the State were to stand aside from all religious institutions, aiding Grangedale in view of its rigidly lay character but refusing to put out fires at St. Swithin's, would the State be discriminating against the church school because of its religious character and so violating the canon of equality proclaimed by the Fourteenth Amendment? The lay State has its problems.

In 1940 the Supreme Court of the United States made

a momentous pronouncement in a case not involving schools but ultimately carrying much influence in school cases. *Cantwell v. Connecticut*[36] arose out of the prosecution of an evangelist, a Jehovah's Witness, for a statutory offense, soliciting funds for a religious cause without a license, and for a common-law offense of inciting a breach of the peace. The Court reversed Cantwell's conviction on both counts. Mr. Justice Roberts, in the opinion, wrote: "The First Amendment declares that Congress shall make no law respecting an establishment of religion or prohibiting the free exercise thereof. The Fourteenth Amendment has rendered the legislatures of the states as incompetent as Congress to enact such laws."[37]

This pronouncement, one notes with some surprise, goes beyond Madison's proposed amendment on state violations of "equal rights of conscience," which the Congress rejected in 1789. Three difficulties arise in the theory of "literal incorporation" of the First Amendment in the Fourteenth, a doctrine now accepted by the Supreme Court; one difficulty is historical, one textual, and one involves practical application. Scrupulous scholarly research of the records concerning the adoption of the Fourteenth Amendment discloses no such intent by the draftsmen, the Congress, or the ratifying States.[38] This, to be sure, should not be conclusive against "incorporation" if the words of the Fourteenth Amendment pre-

[36]310 U.S. 296 (1940).

[37]*Ibid.,* p. 303.

[38]See Charles Fairman and Stanley Morrison, "Does the Fourteenth Amendment Incorporate the Bill of Rights?" 2 *Stanford Law Review* 5 (1949).

scribe it. But the words seem ill adapted to that end. The Due Process and Equal Protection Clauses seem in terms to forbid state tyranny of any sort, to pledge use of the national government's power to prevent any State from undue oppression of anyone. No State, one can easily see, is permitted to deny due process and equal protection to any man by penalizing him on account of his religion. But are the relevant words of the Fourteenth Amendment—"nor shall any State deprive any person of life, liberty, or property, without due process of law; nor deny to any person within its jurisdiction the equal protection of the laws"—really appropriate to mean "no State shall make any law respecting an establishment of religion" in a case where no oppression of any dissenting individual appears? Is the language of the Fourteenth Amendment aptly drawn to forbid any State support for any religion, or even for all of them; does it expressly forbid, share and share alike, any arrangement such as that proposed in 1784 by the Virginia Bill for "establishing a provision for Teachers of the Christian Religion"? Perhaps the question is illusory. Any public aid to pious uses costs money provided by taxpayers, and this compulsion to pay may be considered deprivation of property in violation of the vague canons of due process and equal protection of the laws.

Thus the historic and textual problems of "incorporation" are puzzling enough, but the Supreme Court has got past them, despite considerable contrary outcry, and very likely its rulings are in accord with what most Americans think just and wise. But the practical difficulties are immense in seeking to apply a rule of total disestablishment to the manifold activities which a modern State conducts for the general welfare of its people. The

State wishes to educate its children and to protect them from the hazards of highway travel on foot; may it constitutionally provide busrides to and from school at public cost, knowing, as state authorities do, that some children will certainly go to parochial schools, and that transportation for them will to some extent aid those schools and so aid, a little, the religious indoctrination to which those schools aspire? No one in our time expects to see the legislature in Trenton establish a "State Church of New Jersey"; but is the advantage to a church which school buses give sufficient to constitute an "establishment"? The Fourteenth Amendment, the Court has told us, does not forbid a State to spend money for the transportation of pupils to public and parochial schools alike.[39] But to meet the desires of most of the parents, a school board in Champaign, Illinois, invites unpaid teachers of the Catholic, Jewish, and Protestant faiths to meet on public-school premises for one period of instruction each week those children of their several faiths whose parents wish it. A dissenting child is excused. Is this instruction an "establishment of religion" forbidden by the Due Process and Equal Protection Clauses of the Fourteenth Amendment? If the dissenting child, or his parents, believe religious doctrines different from those expounded by the visiting teacher, or believe none at all, does the necessity of claiming the right to leave the classroom embarrass the dissenter and so impede his free exercise of religion? The Supreme Court in 1948, on the suit of Mrs. Vashti McCollum, a convinced atheist and mother of a child in the Champaign schools, held

[39]Everson v. Board of Education, 330 U.S. 1 (1947). In the prevailing opinion in this case, Mr. Justice Black wrote the words quoted on the first page of this essay.

the instruction unconstitutional, though the ground of its decision—a state "establishment," or hardship on the religious dissenter, or both—is not clear.[40]   This lack of clarity was not eliminated in 1952 when the Supreme Court upheld the constitutionality of excusing from classes for designated periods those public-school children whose parents wished them to go to religious centers away from the school premises for instruction and whose presence at this instruction was demonstrated by certificate of the pastor or other religious teacher.[41]   The prevailing and dissenting opinions of the Justices in this *Zorach* case point up the centuries-old tension among our people, between those who recognize the force of religious concepts in society and wish to have the young turned in their direction and those, on the other hand, who are so profoundly stirred by the necessity of keeping government and religion separate that to this constitutional end they feel compelled to sacrifice the advantage which could come to religious guidance by intermingling it with public schooling.   Justice Douglas wrote in his opinion upholding "released time" for religious instruction:

We are a religious people whose institutions presuppose a Supreme Being. We guarantee the freedom to worship as one chooses. We make room for as wide a variety of beliefs and creeds as the spiritual needs of men deem necessary. We sponsor an attitude on the part of government that shows no partiality . . . . When the state encourages religious instruction or cooperates with religious authorities by adjusting the schedule of public

[40]Illinois *ex rel.* McCollum v. Board of Education, 333 U.S. 203 (1948).

[41]Zorach v. Clauson, 343 U.S. 306 (1952).

events to sectarian needs, it follows the best of our traditions. For it then respects the religious nature of our people and accommodates the public service to their spiritual needs. To hold that it may not would be to find in the Constitution a requirement that the government show a callous indifference to religious groups.[42]

Justices Frankfurter, Black, and Jackson dissented, finding "released time" a violation of the Fourteenth Amendment. Justice Jackson wrote:

The greater effectiveness of this system over voluntary attendance after school hours is due to the truant officer who, if the youngster fails to go to the Church school, dogs him back to the public schoolroom. Here schooling is more or less suspended during the "released time" so that nonreligious attendants will not forge ahead of the church-going absentees. But it serves as a temporary jail for the pupil who will not go to Church. It takes more subtlety of mind than I possess to deny that this is governmental constraint in support of religion.[43]

There is always another river to cross. In many public-school systems the authorities have prescribed that the day's instruction begin by repetition of a brief prayer, often the Lord's Prayer, or by reading a few verses of Scripture, or both. Unfortunately there are different versions of each, identified with different branches of Christianity and inconsistent with Judaism. All, if used as liturgy rather than literary instruction, are unwelcome to atheists. The bystander may wonder why for any of these sectaries a brief exercise desired by a local majority is worth the trouble of litigious opposition. But Justice Frankfurter quotes an English commentator on our

[42]*Ibid.*, pp. 313-14.
[43]*Ibid.*, p. 324 (dissenting opinion).

customs who has pointed out a long-established trait of our people:

At the first sound of a new argument over the United States Constitution and its interpretation the hearts of Americans leap with a fearful joy. The blood stirs powerfully in their veins and a new lustre brightens their eyes. Like King Harry's men before Harfleur, they stand like greyhounds in the slips, straining upon the start.[44]

Anyone who has met the matter of Church and State in political practice knows how close under the surface of human impassivity lie combustible emotions remaining from centuries of traditionally remembered grievances, having causes much more deep than a few minutes of perfunctory religiosity in a classroom morning. A symbol can move us as urgently as substance.

The New York State Board of Regents administers the public-school system of that State. Recognizing the opposing pulls of desired religion for the young, the aspiration to equality before the law, and the constitutional mandate for disestablishment, the Regents undertook the composition of a "nonsectarian" prayer, which should be consistent with the wishes of all religious men. The Regents, in a small way, were thus aspiring to what the sponsors of "A Bill establishing a provision for Teachers of the Christian Religion" had hoped to accomplish in 1784. The Regents' Prayer read: "Almighty God, we acknowledge our dependence upon Thee, and we beg Thy blessings upon us, our parents, our teachers and our Country."[45]

[44]Youngstown Sheet & Tube Co. v. Sawyer, 343 U.S. 579, 594 (1952), quoting from *The Economist,* May 10, 1952, p. 37.

[45]This prayer is quoted in Engel v. Vitale, 370 U.S. 421, 422 (1962).

The twenty-two words require about twelve seconds to read with reverent slowness. The Regents recommended but did not require repetition of this prayer in public schools. The school board in New Hyde Park, New York, directed its teachers to use the prayer but permitted pupils to absent themselves by parental arrangement and directed: "Neither teachers nor any school authority shall comment on participation or non-participation . . . nor suggest or request that any posture or language be used or dress be worn or be not used or not worn."[46] The constraint on a child who disagrees, or whose parent disagrees, with the exercise seems pretty slight, but the "establishment" was sufficient to bring a majority of the Supreme Court, on the complaint of some parents of pupils, to condemn the Regents' Prayer as a violation of the Fourteenth Amendment "incorporating" the First. Justice Black, writing the majority opinion, concedes that this demonstration of schoolroom piety is comparatively trifling: "[I]ndeed, the governmental endorsement of that prayer seems relatively insignificant when compared to the governmental encroachments upon religion which were commonplace 200 years ago."[47]

But he answers this argument *de minimis* by a quotation from Madison's "Remonstrance" of 1784:

[I]t is proper to take alarm at the first experiment on our liberties. . . . Who does not see that the same authority which can establish Christianity, in exclusion of all other Religions, may establish with the same ease any particular sect of Christians, in exclusion of all other Sects? That the same authority which can force a citizen to contribute three pence only of his property for the

[46]*Ibid.,* p. 438 (Douglas, J., concurring).

[47]*Ibid.,* p. 436.

support of any one establishment, may force him to conform to any other establishment in all cases whatsoever?[48]

After the *Regents' Prayer Case,* there was little surprise when in 1963 the Supreme Court found similarly unconstitutional the use of the Lord's Prayer and Bible reading in public schools.[49] Bible reading introduces another complication, however. Suppose that a high school, wishing to inculcate a sense of the majesty of our ancestors' English, uses the King James version of the Bible as the subject of language study, not for the purpose of liturgical ceremony. Does the worthy motive of literacy outweigh the constitutional proscription of publicly supported piety? The question is entirely practical. In a large American city, a high-school principal recently instituted a course in the history of western civilization. The instruction was given to students selected for unusual intelligence; readings of college-level books were prescribed, all after the most advanced pedagogical ideas. A book used in the course and supplied at public expense discussed, among other matters, the origins of Christianity in our civilization. It was a noted work, written by distinguished university scholars; it was not irreverent or iconoclastic, but it did discuss Church beginnings in a spirit of lay historical scholarship rather than as a matter of supernatural intervention. Some students, unused to this type of study, told their parents; the startled parents complained to their parish clergy; a delegation of the clergy waited upon the unhappy principal to protest that the doctrines of their Church were for churchly, not lay academic, exposition and that perchance the principal

[48]*Ibid.*

[49]School District v. Schempp, together with Murray v. Curlett, 374 U.S. 203 (1963).

might by his instruction offend one of their little ones.
The principal called in the books and directed that the
offending chapter be cut from the text.

There is much to be said for the worthy pedagogue's
discreet position. The content of education in tax-sup-
ported institutions may well be controlled, within constitutional limits, by the officers selected, mediately or im-
mediately by political and therefore majoritarian proc-
esses, to conduct that education. Controversies over
religious matters are inevitably divisive. To equip the
young with the undisputed parts of man's history is a
sufficient task without undertaking to engage them in
religious disputation. *De fide non disputandum.* Still,
where shall one stop? Shall the young be told of the
Council of Trent? How? That there was much, or
something, to be said on both sides? The concession of
arguability may by itself be damaging to some young
person's faith. The history book, which the good principal proposed to censor with razor blades, presented a
question customarily a matter of faith, of authoritative
doctrine, as though it were a question answerable by
human scholars reading old manuscripts and unearthing
ancient scrolls, without the aid of supernatural inspira-
tion or belief. This heresy, supported by the ponderous
apparatus of classroom explication, periodic examina-
tions, grades, and backed by the prestigious names of
distinguished occupants of chairs of history in noted universities, becomes much more unsettling to public-school
children than a twelve-second, twenty-two-word, least-
common-denominator prayer could be. There is, indeed,
much to be said for the principal's decision to delete and
forget. *Quae disputanda sunt delenda sunt.*

Unfortunately, he had reckoned without a national
society devoted to civil liberty, of which a chapter

flourished in his city, and he had reckoned without the School Committee, the policy board governing public education in that city, the unfortunate principal's superior authority. At the suggestion of mutilating scholarly books to censor controversial material, the society of civil libertarians, again sensing a new argument over the United States Constitution, felt their hearts again leap with a fearful joy; again they stood like greyhounds in the slips, straining upon the start. They descended upon the School Committtee with eloquent talk of the First Amendment (incorporated, of course, in the Fourteenth). The School Committee saw the point and directed the unhappy principal of their high school to spare those books, cut not a single page.

One regrets to report that this great constitutional issue did not produce a sweeping opinion of the Supreme Court telling the American people what to do about public instruction in matters of history, literature, philosophy, biology, or whatnot, which are all rich in religiously controversial doctrine. The parties seem to have abandoned the matter; it briefly appears in, and then entirely disappears from, the newspapers of the troubled city.

This unlitigated case has overtones of an earlier dispute, actually litigated in Tennessee in 1925. The legislature of that State, troubled by scientists' doctrines of evolution which cast doubt on the account of creation in the Book of Genesis, had enacted a statute which provided:

⌈I⌉t shall be unlawful for any teacher in any of the Universities, Normals and all other public schools of the State which are supported in whole or in part by the public schools funds of the State, to teach any theory that denies the story of the Divine Creation of man as taught in the Bible, and to teach instead that man has descended from a lower order of animals.[50]

A young biology teacher at the Central High School of Dayton, Tennessee, named John Thomas Scopes, to test the validity of the statute, taught the evolution of man in his school and was arrested. William Jennings Bryan, former Secretary of State, thrice Democratic nominee for the Presidency, volunteered his services as counsel for the prosecution. Friends of Scopes secured for the defense the services of Clarence Darrow, a famous Chicago trial lawyer, Dudley Field Malone, and Arthur Garfield Hays. Dayton, Tennessee, became a center of news services. Scopes was found guilty and fined one hundred dollars. The State Supreme Court reversed this conviction on a technicality, without declaring the antievolution statute unconstitutional. Scopes, thus not aggrieved by a conviction, could not carry his case to the Supreme Court of the United States.[51]

There are, of course, differences between the *Regents' Prayer Case* and the Scopes Trial. The Tennessee statute forbade a specified controversial indoctrination; the New York Regents authorized another. Perhaps the Tennessee legislators were commanding their public-school teachers to be inactively neutral on a doctrinal question, while the New Hyde Park school board was commanding its teachers to act, and to act nonneutrally, on a doctrinal matter. The Supreme Court directed the New Hyde Park teachers to desist and be silent on matters of religious doctrine. This, the Court said, is our Constitu-

[50] *Tennessee Acts 1925,* ch. 27, pp. 50-51.

[51] A vivid account of the Scopes Trial appears in Frederick Lewis Allen's *Only Yesterday* (New York, 1931), pp. 201-6.

tion's command in matters of Church and State.

Because of the long religious habit of our people, a hermetic sealing off of each, Church and State, is a difficult and intricate process. Justice Robert Jackson wisely wrote in his concurring opinion in the *McCollum* case:

I think it remains to be demonstrated whether it is possible, even if desirable, . . . completely to isolate and cast out of secular education all that some people may reasonably regard as religious instruction. Perhaps subjects such as mathematics, physics or chemistry are, or can be, completely secularized. But it would not seem practical to teach either practice or appreciation of the arts if we are to forbid exposure of youth to any religious influences. Music without sacred music, architecture minus the cathedral, or painting without the scriptural themes would be eccentric and incomplete, even from a secular point of view. Yet the inspirational appeal of religion in these guises is often stronger than in forthright sermon. Even such a "science" as biology raises the issue between evolution and creation as an explanation of our presence on this planet. Certainly a course in English literature that omitted the Bible and other powerful uses of our mother tongue for religious ends would be pretty barren. And I should suppose it is a proper, if not an indispensable, part of preparation for a worldly life to know the roles that religion and religions have played in the tragic story of mankind. The fact is that, for good or for ill, nearly everything in our culture worth transmitting, everything which gives meaning to life, is saturated with religious influences, derived from paganism, Judaism, Christianity—both Catholic and Protestant—and other faiths accepted by a large part of the world's peoples. One can hardly respect a system of education that would leave the student wholly ignorant of the currents of religious thought that move the world society for a part in which he is being prepared.

But how one can teach, with satisfaction or even with justice to all faiths, such subjects as the story of the Reformation, the Inquisition, or even the New England effort to found "a Church without a Bishop and a State without a King," is more than I know. It is too much to expect that mortals will teach subjects about which their contemporaries have passionate controversies with the detachment they may summon to teaching about remote subjects such as Confucius or Mohammed. When instruction turns to proselyting and imparting knowledge becomes evangelism is, except in the crudest cases, a subtle inquiry.[52]

This essay has surveyed in superficial brevity a long road across seven and one-half centuries, the course of our people's ideas as to the just relation between "the Church" and "the State." In 1215 the Christian Church could reasonably assert its unity throughout western Europe. The great schism of 1054 had divided the Eastern Church from that of Rome, but from the Baltic to Gibraltar, from the southern tip of Sicily to the far northwest of Ireland, men acknowledged the same spiritual leader in Rome and felt that they all belonged to one great organic whole Church, whether they gave feudal allegiance to an overlord in the places we now call Germany, or France, or Italy, or Spain, or Scotland, or Ireland, or England. A dreaded papal interdict could suspend most religious services in any part of that area; a man cut off from the rites of his Church might face excommunication with outward bravado, but he became a sort of religious outlaw and he must have felt awe in his soul. Church dignitaries exercised much of what we now think of as lay government, and continual disputes

[52]333 U.S. at 235-36 (concurring opinion).

went on as to the respective parts played by feudal monarch and by Pope in selecting these churchly magnates. In contests between monarch and Church, the Church was apt to win, as Henry found out when his men murdered Becket in 1170, and as John discovered between 1207 and 1213 when he tried to oppose Innocent's choice of Stephen Langton as Archbishop of Canterbury. Meantime lowly men subsisted on the uncertain harvest of the common field, took no part in the choice of their rulers, either lay or spiritual, and hoped only to fall afoul of no cruel magnate.

One need not take sides in any doctrinal controversy to conclude that, in the course of seven centuries, the organized Church, compared to organized government, has come to play a greatly diminished part in most men's lives. So to conclude, we need only believe expressions of sorrow on that subject from notable churchmen. In 1215 the word "State," if it or any word like it was heard at all, carried no meaning for the hearer such as today is carried by the names "France," "Germany," "China," "Italy," "Great Britain," or the "United States." And to speak of "the Church" connotes quite different matters in our time. What Church? Respected and revered as the Roman Catholic Church is, its most devoted members must concede that the confusion of assorted Christian churches in Europe and America is inconsistent with any such position of single authority as Innocent III occupied in 1215. The thunder of interdicts no longer terrifies England. Excommunication of the Prime Minister of England as a measure of international relations now seems unlikely, no matter what the political controversy may be. Whatever "the Church" may now mean, the most powerful judicial tribunal in the world has ruled that lest religion ally itself with government in the smallest degree, a schoolteacher in a state-maintained school in suburban New York must not utter a twenty-two-word prayer to which, by regulation, no pupil need give attention anyway. Church is not the Church it was in 1215; our State is a phenomenon which did not then exist. Today's world would bewilder the magnates of feudal nobility and of the ancient Church who warily parleyed and then made a great compact in the meadow at Runnymede.